Our Government

The Three Branches

Shelly Buchanan, M.S.Ed.

Consultant

Caryn Williams, M.S.Ed.
Madison County Schools
Huntsville, AL

Image Credits: Cover & p.1 Pgiam/iStock; p.4 Dave Pattison/Alamy; p.14 nsf/Alamy; p.9 (top) J. Scott Applewhite/Associated Press; p.29 (bottom) Ron Edmonds/Associated Press; p.17 Everett Collection/Newscom; pp.24–25 (background) Alex Wong/Getty Images; p.15 Dirck Halstead/Time Life Pictures/Getty Images; p.27 Washington Post/Getty Images; p.6 Washington Post/Getty Images; p.12 The Granger Collection, NYC/The Granger Collection; p.5 HultonArchive/iStock; p.10 (left) LOC, LC-DIG-hec-35541; p.16 (bottom) LOC, LC-USZ62-7449 The Library of Congress; p.23 (right) Dennis Brack bb37/Newscom; pp.8–9 (background) Jim Lo Scalzo/EPA/Newscom; p.18 Martin H. Simon/UPI/Newscom; p.11 Scott J. Ferrell/ Congressional Quarterly/Newscom; p.19 (bottom) ZUMA Press/Newscom; pp.20–21 (top & right) North Wind Picture Archives; p.25 (top) The U.S. National Archives; pp.7, p.10 (right), p.13, p.19 (top), p.22, p.23 (left), pp.28–29 Wikimedia Commons; all other images from Shutterstock.

Library of Congress Cataloging-in-Publication Data

Buchanan, Shelly.
  Our government: the three branches / Shelly Buchanan, M.S.Ed.
    pages cm
  Includes index.
  ISBN 978-1-4333-7365-7 (pbk.)
  ISBN 978-1-4807-5151-4 (ebook)
1. United States—Politics and government—Juvenile literature. 2. Separation of powers—United States—Juvenile literature. I. Title.
  JK40.B84 2014
  320.473—dc23

2014010577

Teacher Created Materials

5301 Oceanus Drive
Huntington Beach, CA 92649-1030
http://www.tcmpub.com
ISBN 978-1-4333-7365-7

© 2015 Teacher Created Materials, Inc.
Printed in China
Nordica.012019.CA21801586

Table of Contents

A New Country Is Born 4

Separation of Powers 6

The Legislative Branch 8

The Executive Branch 14

The Judicial Branch 20

Justice for All 27

Write It! 28

Glossary 30

Index 31

Your Turn! 32

A New Country Is Born

In 1783, America won a war against Great Britain. It was now its own country. It was finally free! This new country would be called the *United States of America*.

The early leaders of America knew that they needed a strong government to be in charge of the whole country. They needed it to help the states and to keep them safe.

The leaders met in Philadelphia (fil-uh-DEL-fee-uh). They wanted to create a **democracy** (dih-MOK-ruh-see). This is when everyone has a voice and a **vote**. They did not want one person to have too much power. The U.S. Constitution (kon-sti-TOO-shuhn) would explain how all this should work.

Leaders met in Independence Hall in Philadelphia.

George Washington returns to New York after winning the war.

The American Revolution

Americans did not like being ruled by the king of Great Britain. They thought he was unfair. So they went to war to be free. This war is known as the *American Revolution*. George Washington led the American Army during the American Revolution.

Separation of Powers

The U.S. Constitution is the main set of laws for our country. It says how our government should work. It also lists all the things Americans can do and should have. These are called *rights*.

The U.S. Constitution says that the government should be split into three branches, or parts. Each branch has its own jobs and makes big decisions. One branch always checks the work of the other two branches. This system is called *checks and balances*. It keeps one branch from having too much power. The branches work together and protect the rights of the people.

President George W. Bush signs a law in 2008.

Checks and Balances

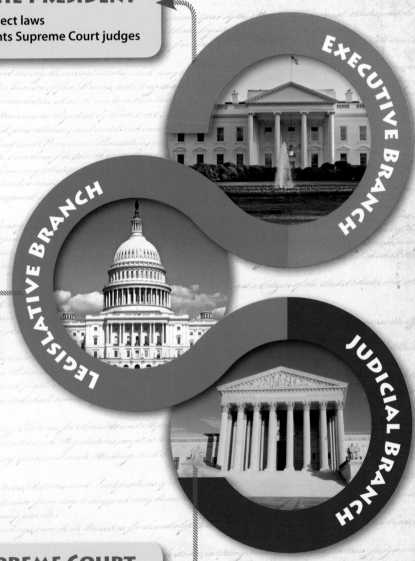

THE PRESIDENT
- Can reject laws
- Appoints Supreme Court judges

EXECUTIVE BRANCH

CONGRESS
- Can reject president's ruling
- Can limit spending of federal money
- Can remove the president

LEGISLATIVE BRANCH

JUDICIAL BRANCH

SUPREME COURT
- Can throw out laws that are unconstitutional

The Legislative Branch

The legislative branch is made up of two groups. One group is the House of **Representatives** (rep-ri-ZEN-tuh-tivs), or simply the *House*. The other group is the Senate. Together, they are known as Congress. Congress is made up of leaders from each state.

The U.S. Constitution explains the job of Congress. Its biggest job is to make laws. This helps our government run smoothly. The laws let the government collect **taxes**. These taxes pay for the government. They pay for new roads and bridges. They also pay for our **armed forces**. These are our soldiers who keep our country safe.

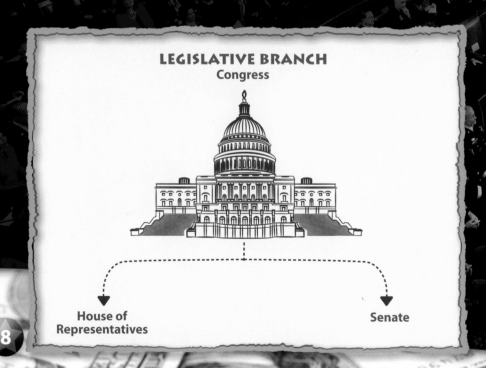

LEGISLATIVE BRANCH
Congress

House of
Representatives

Senate

Money Makers

Congress is also in charge of printing our money. Before the U.S. Constitution, each state made its own money. This was very confusing! Today, all Americans use the same money.

President Obama speaks to Congress.

The House of Representatives

The House is much larger than the Senate. Each state sends representatives to the House. Larger states send more people. Smaller states send fewer people. This means that bigger states have more power in the House.

Each member in the House **represents** an area of his or her state. People in each area choose the member by voting. Today, there are 435 members in the House.

The members serve for two years in the House. When their two years are up, the people in the members' states vote. They can vote to keep the same representatives, or they can vote for new ones.

The House makes laws about taxes. It also decides if a member should be removed from the House. This can happen if people think the member broke a law.

Edith Nourse Rogers becomes the first woman to lead a session in the House of Representatives in 1929.

Rules to Be a Representative

To be a representative, you have to be at least 25 years old. You also need to have been a U.S. **citizen** for at least seven years. And you have to be living in the state you want to represent.

Members of the House of Representatives pose for a picture on the steps of the U.S. Capitol.

11

The Senate

Like the House, the Senate is made up of representatives from each state. But the Senate only has two members from each state. So each state has the same power in the Senate.

There are 100 members of the Senate. Each member can serve for six years. The people can then vote for that member to stay, or they can vote for a new member.

The U.S. Senate in session in 1836.

The Senate of the United States.

The Senate does important work. It looks at **treaties** the president makes. These are agreements with other countries. The Senate has the final say on these treaties. It also votes on people the president wants to hire.

U. S. Senate, 2010

Rules to Be a Senator

To be a senator, you must be at least 30 years old. You also need to have been a U.S. citizen for at least nine years. And you have to be living in the state you want to represent.

The Executive Branch

The president is America's top leader. He or she leads the executive branch. This is a big job. About four million people work for this branch!

The president makes sure our country runs smoothly. He or she must follow the rules in the U.S. Constitution. For example, the president cannot pass a new law alone. First, Congress has to agree that it should be a law. Then, it can be passed. This is a rule in the Constitution.

President Ronald Reagan signs a new law.

There are a lot of people who help the president. They are called the *cabinet*. The cabinet helps run different parts of the government. It also keeps the president informed. It tells him or her about events in the world. This helps the president work with leaders in other countries.

Rules to Be the President

To be the president, you must be 35 years old. You must be a citizen who was born in the United States. And you must have lived in the United States for at least 14 years.

President Bill Clinton is sworn in as the 42nd president of the United States.

Presidents represent our country in world matters. This means that they travel a lot! They tour the world to meet with other leaders. They try to keep the peace. They make plans for the future.

The president is also the Commander-in-Chief. This means that he or she is in charge of the armed forces. The president can send them to other countries. But Congress has to agree to send soldiers to fight. The president is not allowed to start a war on his or her own. Only Congress can send the country to war. This keeps the president from being too powerful.

Flying High

When the president travels, he or she flies on Air Force One. This is a special plane made just for the president.

President Roosevelt (ROH-zuh-velt) (bottom, middle) meets with world leaders to discuss peace during World War II.

President George H. W. Bush has Thanksgiving dinner with U.S. troops in 1990.

President Barack Obama
signs a bill into law.

In America, people choose the president by voting. The person who gets the most votes becomes the new president. This happens every four years. A person can be president only twice. This means that no one can be president for more than eight years.

The president works closely with Congress. Congress passes **bills**. Each bill then goes to the president. He or she may sign the bill. This makes the bill a law. The president can also send the bill back to Congress to be changed. Or the president may **veto** the bill. A veto means that the bill is rejected. This keeps Congress from being too powerful. It is part of the checks and balances system.

Vice President

The vice president is also part of the executive branch. The vice president's main job is to take over if the president is no longer able to do his or her job.

Vice President Joe Biden

President Obama's signature

The Judicial Branch

The Supreme Court leads the judicial branch. It is the highest court in the country. It is in charge of all the courts. The Supreme Court hears the biggest cases in America. It listens to people who do not agree on something. Then, it makes a decision about what the law says. This is called a **ruling**. All courts must follow what the Supreme Court says. Its rulings become the law.

The Supreme Court tries to treat all people fairly. The Supreme Court judges are called **justices**. They choose about 100 cases to hear each year. They make rulings based on the U.S. Constitution.

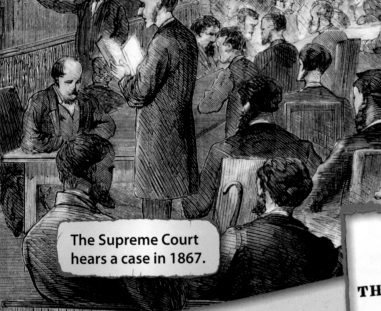

The Supreme Court hears a case in 1867.

Supreme Court building

U.S. Supreme Court case

THE CASE

OF

THE CHEROKEE NATION

against

THF STATE OF GEORGIA:

ARGUED AND DETERMINED AT

THE SUPREME COURT OF THE UNITED STATES,

JANUARY TERM 1831.

WITH

AN APPENDIX,

Containing the Opinion of Chancellor Kent on the Case; the Treaties between the United States and the Cherokee Indians; the Act of Congress of 1802, entitled 'An Act to regulate intercourse with the Indian tribes, &c.'; and the Laws of Georgia relative to the country occupied by the Cherokee Indians, within the boundary of that State.

BY RICHARD PETERS,

COUNSELLOR AT LAW.

Philadelphia:
JOHN GRIGG, 9 NORTH FOURTH STREET.
1831.

The president picks the Supreme Court justices. There are nine in all. One is the chief justice. He or she leads the Supreme Court. Most justices have worked as lawyers. Lawyers represent people in court, and try to help them win a case. Some justices have even served in other branches of the government.

Supreme Court Justices, 2014

Sonia Sotomayor
(soh-toh-my-YOR)
(since 2009)

Stephen Breyer
(BRAHY-er)
(since 1994)

Samuel Alito Jr.
(uh-LEE-toh)
(since 2006)

Elena Kagan
(KAY-guhn)
(since 2010)

Ruth Ginsburg
(GINZ-burg)
(since 1993)

Clarence Thomas
(since 1991)

John Roberts Jr.
(since 2005)

Anthony Kennedy
(since 1988)

Antonin Scalia
(skuh-LEE-uh)
(since 1986)

Thurgood Marshall

Sandra Day O'Connor

There is no limit for how long a justice can serve. This means that he or she may serve on the court for life. A justice can quit or **retire**. If they do something wrong, they may be taken off the court.

There have been more than 100 justices. In 1967, Thurgood Marshall was the first African American justice. In 1981, Sandra Day O'Connor was the first woman justice. Today, there are three women justices.

Justice Kagan is sworn in on Capitol Hill in 2010.

The Supreme Court makes sure that the other two branches are doing their jobs. It checks to see if they are following the U.S. Constitution. This is part of the checks and balances system.

The Nineteenth Amendment gave women the right to vote.

Sixty-sixth Congress of the United States of America;

At the First Session,

Begun and held at the City of Washington on Monday, the nineteenth day of May, one thousand nine hundred and nineteen.

JOINT RESOLUTION

Proposing an amendment to the Constitution extending the right of suffrage to women.

Resolved by the Senate and House of Representatives of the United States of America in Congress assembled (two-thirds of each House concurring therein), That the following article is proposed as an amendment to the Constitution, which shall be valid to all intents and purposes as part of the Constitution when ratified by the legislatures of three-fourths of the several States.

" ARTICLE ————.

"The right of citizens of the United States to vote shall not be denied or abridged by the United States or by any State on account of sex.

"Congress shall have power to enforce this article by appropriate legislation."

F. H. Gillett.

Speaker of the House of Representatives.

Thos. R. Marshall.

Vice President of the United States and President of the Senate.

The Supreme Court justices work hard to protect people's rights. They look at laws to make sure they are fair. It is the job of the Supreme Court to say how the law works. If they think that a law goes against the U.S. Constitution or is unfair, it is thrown out. They have the final say on the law. Only an **amendment** to the U.S. Constitution can change a ruling made by the Supreme Court. An amendment is a change to the U.S. Constitution.

People celebrate
America in 2013.

Justice for All

America is more than 200 years old. So is the U.S. Constitution. We have the oldest working constitution in the world. Our early leaders made a strong constitution. It formed a government with three branches. The three branches check and balance one another. This way, one person or group does not have too much power.

In the future, America will face new challenges. The Constitution will change. The three branches of government will change, too. Our laws may change. New laws will be added. But there will still be a balance of power. The branches will try to treat all people fairly. There will always be **justice** for all.

Siblings lead the Pledge of Allegiance on the anniversary of the signing of the U.S. Constitution.

Write It!

Learn about your local government leaders. Write a letter to a member of the Senate or the House. Or write a letter to a local judge! Tell him or her what you think about our country. Explain what kinds of laws you think our country needs. Talk about the changes you would make to our country. Ask him or her any questions you have about our government.

Kids write letters to government leaders about many things.

Dear Senator Boxer:

Hi, my name is Maria Ross and I am studying US History. I am an third grade student at Hilton School in San Los Angeles. We have been studying the political progress and the Constitution. I am writing to you to discuss your views and voting on issues that pertain to fighting at school. I think fighting is bad and that you should reconsider your views.

Your sincerely,

U.S. Capitol building

Congress in session

Glossary

amendment—a change to the words or meaning of a law or document

armed forces—the military organizations of a country

bills—written descriptions of new laws

citizen—a person who legally belongs to a country

democracy—a form of government in which people choose leaders by voting

justice—the process of using laws to judge fairly

justices—judges in the Supreme Court

representatives—people who speak or act for someone officially

represents—speaks or acts for someone or something officially

retire—to stop doing a job because you have reached an age when you do not need to or want to work

ruling—an official decision made by a judge

taxes—an amount of money that people pay to the government

treaties—official agreements that are made between two or more countries

veto—to reject officially

vote—to make an official choice for or against someone or something

Index

Alito, Samuel, Jr., 22

Biden, Joe, 19

Breyer, Stephen, 22

Bush, George W., 6

Bush, George, H. W., 17

Clinton, Bill, 15

Congress, 7–9, 14, 16, 19, 29

Ginsburg, Ruth, 22

House of Representatives, 8, 10–11, 28

Kagan, Elena, 22, 24

Kennedy, Anthony, 22

Marshall, Thurgood, 23

Obama, Barack, 9, 18–19

O'Connor, Sandra 23

Roberts, John, Jr., 22

Rodgers, Edith Nourse, 10

Roosevelt, Franklin, 16

Scalia, Antonin, 22

Senate, 8, 10, 12–13, 28

Sotomayor, Sonia, 22

Thomas, Clarence, 22

U.S. Constitution, 4, 6, 8–9, 14, 20, 24–25, 27

Washington, George, 5

Your Turn!

Which Branch?

Pretend you are going to work for the government. Which branch do you want to work for? What job do you want to do? Write a list of pros and cons for different jobs to help you decide.